Fairie-ality

Spring. . . . the word itself sounds zesty. Like something exciting's going to happen. It's my favourite time of year and I'll tell you why—it's The Season. Even before last frost, invitations fly in from everywhere for cotillions and concerts, picnics and parades. Midnight games and twilight gambols. Evening flights and daylight rambles. It begins when the bluebells bloom, and by the end, when sun spills into midsummer, the fields are loaded with daisies and roses. The middle is filled with parties and play.

You'll see . . .

Spring . . . the word itself sounds zesty, like something exciting's going to happen. It's my favourite time of year and I'll tell you why—it's The Season. Even before last frost, invitations fly in from everywhere for cotillions and concerts, picnics and parades. Midnight games and twilight gambols. Evening flights and daylight rambles. It begins when the bluebells bloom, and by the end, when sun spills into midsummer, the fields are loaded with daisies and roses. The middle is filled with parties and play.

You'll see . . .

In the fairie world there is one top designer of couture and accessories.

This catalogue brings together his brand-new collection for the very first time . . .

Fairie

-ality

THE

FASHION

COLLECTION

from

THE HOUSE OF LLWAND

THE SEASON approaches, and it gives us the greatest pleasure to present the new spring line from the renowned House of Ellwand. Addressing all your requirements, from impeccably tailored flywear for urban and field outings to elegant ball gowns and eveningwear—not to mention the freshest visions in unmentionables—the celebrated *couturier* conjures fabrics from fantasy and dresses from dreams.

Ellwand keeps his *atelier* in the ancient bluebell groves of West Sussex. Outside, a tiny unmarked door offers no sign to passersby, for the creator needs his privacy. Inside, masses of wildflowers, dried grasses, feathers and seedpods, pine cones and polished pretties surround the designer as he works late into the night, turning his passionate visions into one-of-a-kind realities.

Peek into the pamphlet here for a preview of Ellwand's dazzling creations. This year, for the unwinged, we are pleased to include a line of flight hats. Made to the most stringent design standards, these trendy toppers also provide maximum lift. Indeed, in recent trials, our hats have proven unmatched as flying aids. If you're winged, you won't need our hats for flight, but you'll certainly want them for fashion. Just as many heads will turn!

A final word about your selections. In-country orders will not, of course, require size specifications because of the shape- and size-changing abilities of our clientele. However, international orders must be handled on an individual basis and require an additional two weeks' shipping time.

Those of you who have dealt with us in the past know of our commitment to flexibility and our imaginative openness to the payment process. To those of you joining us for the first time, we say *bienvenue*. We look forward to assisting you.

H.R.F.H. The Queen
requests the pleasure of your company
at the
Cotillion of the Pheasant
on the
First Full Moon
After the Bluebells Bloom

at

Sunset

in

the Oak Grove

The Presentation to The Queen
Will be followed by the Flying Figures,
Dinner, and Dancing

R.S.V.P. Royal Acorn Post

We're leaving now for the Nut Tree Thicket, where the cotillion gowns are awaiting their owners. Each dancer will need a helper to fluff her feathers and adjust the fastenings — my sister Lavinia chose me! At sunset, Lavinia will open the ball by presenting the bluebell nosegay to the Queen, and next, all the girls will perform their flying figures. They must execute them perfectly — a single missed turn or delayed hover could mean catastrophe. Later, after the banquet, we'll all get to dance and fly.

It's going to be a magical night!

At the Pleasure of Her Majesty

Everyone gasped as Violette floated by in her parrot feather gown. She had a way of dancing and flying that caused all the other fairies to stop and stare, though she never seemed to notice.

Violette's Gown

Exotic parrot feathers;
snakeskin belt with red gum seeds.
Skeleton leaf cobwebbing and
simple alder leaf straps on the bodice.
No pheasant for this rebel!

There sleeps Titania

some time of the night,

Lull'd in these flowers

with dances and delight;

And there the snake

throws her enamell'd skin,

Weed wide enough to

wrap a fairy in.

Titania Gown

The Bard himself could not have thought up the unlikely,
skin-tingling combination of pigeon (the skirt) and
pheasant (the sleeves) with a constricted snakeskin bodice.

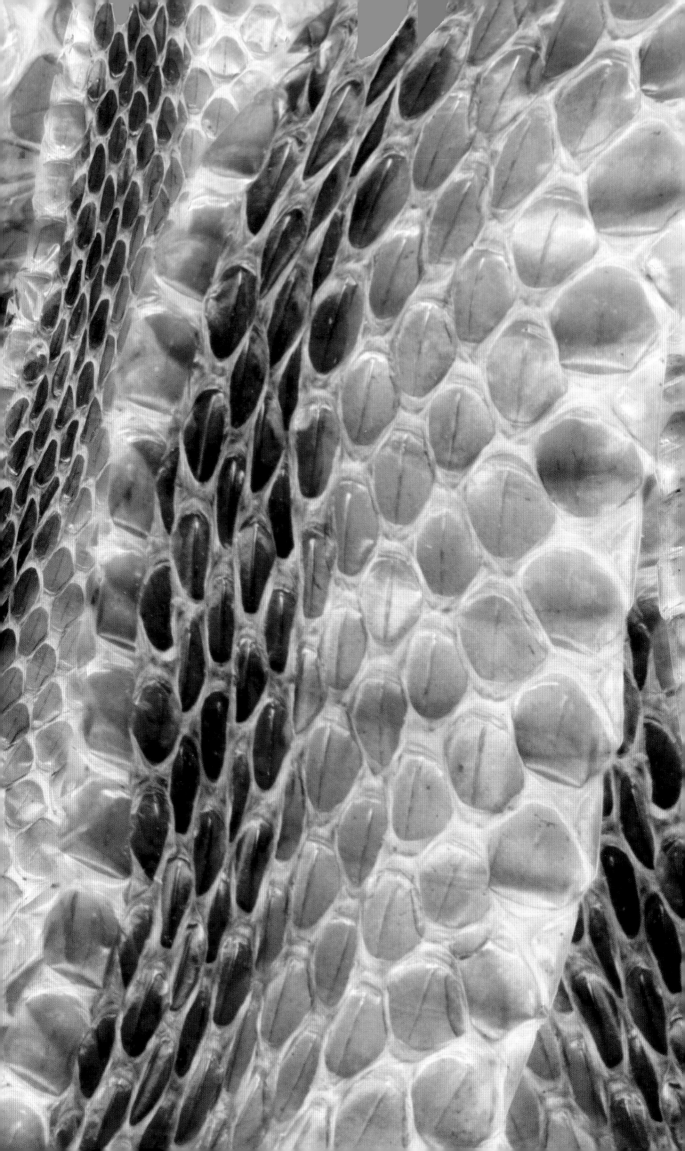

Just shed your snakeskin bodice
to reveal this second skin.

Underwear? Of course.
Swimwear? Why not?

Postmidnight Dip
These splendidly
mentionable unmentionables
are trimmed in honesty seeds.

Who says feathers are just for the birds?

Rara Avis Gown

Iridescent hues of parrot blue and green, intensified by a flick of yellow at the neck and cuff.

Coup de grace

If your own presentation to
the Queen is just a pleasant
memory, but now you're pleasure-
bent, we have the perfect gown.
You were the first in your Cotillion
class yesterday, and you're the
dernier cri today.

Coup de Grace

Shaped parrot feather skirt with strapless bodice of sweet
chestnut and a zigzag of monkey puzzle spikes at the waist.
A jewel in the crown for the sophisticate who's young at heart.

The Streamlined Mule

Just the heel to slip on when you plan to dance and dazzle.
Upper of rose petals with cow parsley seed trim;
birch bark sole.

The Paradox Hat

What emerges from these
ominous roots and bulb
when they're at home?
A cheery crocus! Here
the roots have a firm grip
on lime-green parrot
feathers. To be worn by
those who cherish mystery.

The Pumpkin Zeppelin

The Rose Poppy Topper

The Squirrel's Delight

The Plumed Blimp

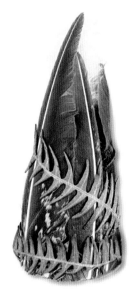

The Fern Frond Mitre

The Baby Beanie

floating and flitting ∞ *airy heights* — ∞ *takeoff* ∞

The Cosmic Pincushion

The Bracken Belfry

The Pheasant Tailwind

The Parrot Mad Hatter

The Pine Needle Shako

The Sycamore Sorcerer

touchdown ❦ *cruising altitude* ❦ *lighter than air*

The Language of Love

Gather the flowers whose sentiments express your message,

placing the most important flower in the center.

Make a collar of lady's mantle or ivy to surround the flowers.

Firmly bind all the stems together with ribbon grass or

feather thread, finishing in a bow.

Secretly place your tussie mussie on the threshold of

your sweetheart's, beau's, or best friend's house—

then fly away so you won't be discovered.

I've been waiting all year for tomorrow—
It's May Day!
Before cockcrow, I'll be picking fresh
buttercups and cowslips, dianthus, violets,
and red currant to make little tussie mussies.
I'll tuck them in
the roots by my
best friends'
houses. I'll weave the
rest of the flowers into a
garland and wear it when
we dance around the
white hawthorn tree.

Bougainvillaea: Elegance

Bridal Wreath: Happiness

Buttercups: Childhood memories

Calla Lily: Female beauty

Columbine: Determined to succeed

Cosmos: May I have the next dance?

Cowslips: Divine beauty

Daisy: Innocence

Dianthus: Make haste

Dock: Patience

Fuchsia: Humble love

Gerbera: Beauty

Hyacinth: Sorrow

Ivy: Marriage

Lady's Mantle: Comfort, protection

Lilac: First love

Lily: Purity

Mint: Virtue

Pansy: You occupy my thoughts

Pinks: Fascination

Queen Anne's Lace: Fantasy

Red Currant: You please me

Red Rose: Love

Violet: Fidelity

The revelry celebrating

High Spring lasts all day,

but at dusk the band packs

up and goes home—

which is perfectly fine

with this pair, who

keep dancing to the

only music they need:

the wild beating of

their own hearts.

Rose Pierrot

Rose petals with pompom of gerbera daisy.

Rose Dance Dress for Her

Luscious sculpted layers of lily and rose petals.
For one with a heart full of passion.

Rose Jacket for Him

Bougainvillaea with Mexican bird of paradise, daisies,
a dusting of Queen Anne's lace, and most important,
rose petal flourishes at cuff and hip.

Made for Each Other

Stargazer Spinning Dress

From the high noon circle dances to an evening comet-counting party, you're queen for a day.

The skirt is a carnival of stargazer lilies; the top, a wrapped lily, secured by narrow lily straps.

When the Rade Passes By

When the royal family passes by in the Fairie Rade, everyone holds still. In the hush, they can hear the wind blowing through the tiny whistles nestled in the horses' manes; the ringle-jingle of the belled bridles; the musical clip-clop of the Lilliputian hooves. The riders' mounts are the colours of a late spring garden: hyacinth, fuchsia, rose, lilac. We like to ensure that our Rade regalia is equally vivid.

Harlequin Dress

Layers of pink dianthus ruffle the frothy skirt of this dress. Bodice and sleeves of piercing fuchsia with a necklace graced by bridal wreath, pinned with a seashell.

The Jockey Jacket and Knee Britches

Brilliant bell-shaped sleeves and trousers of fuchsia. Military rows of stamen fastenings march down the fuchsia leaf vest.

May I request the honour of the next two dances?

(I don't stand a chance.
She's so sophisticated and stunning.
Will she find me too
fiddle-footed and tatty?)

She says —

I am pleased to accept.

(He's so suave and dashing.
Will he think I'm flighty?)

Da

This

lily

self-

Timeless Romance

Vintage roses appliquéd over white lily petals. The lavish lilac hem will whisper when you walk in this enchanted and enchanting Rosebud Gown.

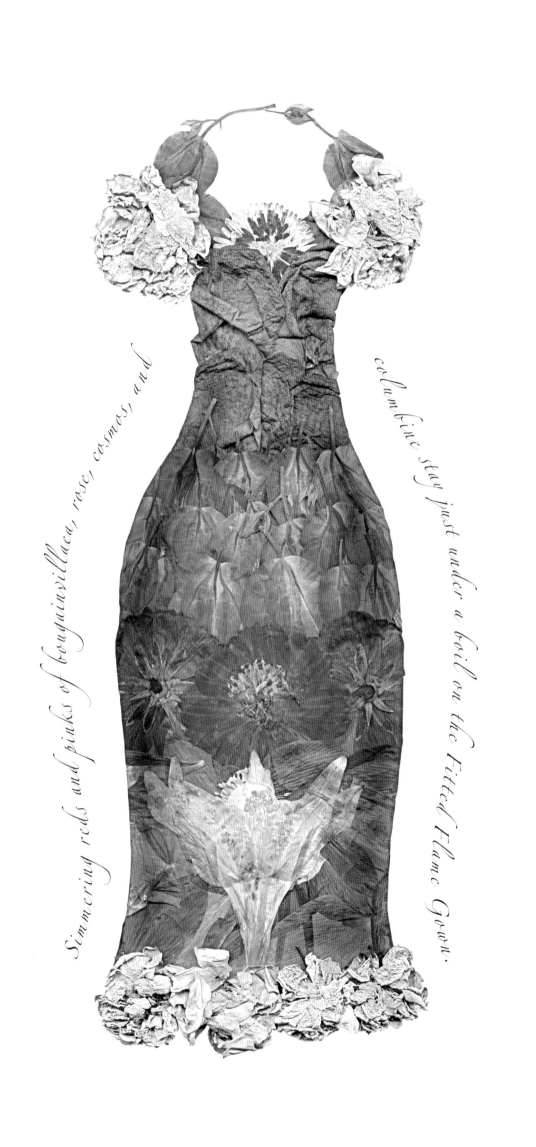

Simmering reds and pinks of bougainvillaea, rose, cosmos, and columbine stay just under a boil on the Fitted Flame Gown.

Our French cousin, Delphine, often visited during The Season and organized impromptu feasts by spreading a rhubarb throw atop a bit of creeping thyme. She served us elegantly on wild-ginger-leaf plates and invited us to sip from her fringed gentian goblets.

Delphine Shirt

Refined rose petal shirt with seed buttons. Timeless, yet up-to-the-minute; suits a *pique-nique*, or a *soirée*, or a *pique-nique soirée*.

Rhubarb Skirt

Wide-wale rhubarb leaves topped with an oak leaf belt, rosebuds, and a red gum seed. Decorous yet earthy.

We were all in awe of Fleur's style, understated and unexpected, though she always included a signature red rose petal somewhere on her clothing.

Fleur Cowl-Necked Shirt

Ivy leaves with overlaid yellow fritillary;
asymmetrical sprays of Queen Anne's lace;
and, naturally, a red rose-petal cowl collar.

A Pansy for Your Thoughts Suit

In the language of flowers, this chic creation is as well thought out as possible. Just the suit to listen to a suite, *alfresco*.

Arabesque Jacket

When you arrive in this concoction of pansies and buttercups with apache plume trim, expect a flattering fanfare.

Late afternoon concertos on the Green. While the panpipe and piccolo solos are the perennial favorites, we would be remiss not to mention the attention paid to the audience. How you are dressed at these events is as carefully noted by your fellow concertgoers as the music. Why not choose elegance? This quartet sets the tone.

The Pansy

Rhapsody Dress

The Rhapsody is also fashioned of pansies and plumes. Like its counterpoint, the Arabesque, it scores high on entrances.

Pastoral Jacket

The theme is pansies but the variation is oak leaf. Restrained, reflective. Don't miss the rose petal lining.

Quartet

THE FAIRIE RADES
DOUBLE DATES
SUNSET PICNICS
HIDE & SEEK
FIREFLY HUNTING
MIDNIGHT DANCING
MOONBEAM SWIMS
MUSICAL EVENINGS
NONSTOP PARTIES

FUN & GAMES

Time to start thinking about afternoon outings
at the falls, long woodland walks, a gathering of friends at the river.
The Season is heating up, and the Ellwand Collection has some of the
coolest looks to throw on as you run off to play.

show a little skin

Tippecanoe Hat Birch bark boater with oak band and a stroke of jay feather.
Hawaiian Skirt Stone pine needles, silver birch belt with shooting stars.
Fill It to the Top Tank A beguiling blue larkspur cooler.
Seashell Sandal Hard to say, but easy to wear. Birch sole, anthurium straps, and shell bauble.

The Mae

Lush crow and owl
feathers, bottlebrush, and
a dash of honesty seeds.

The Marilyn

Lip-smacking pink, red,
and blue verbena with
peacock straps.

The Mata Hari

Mysterious pheasant
with pink rosebuds and
peacock straps.

Bathing Beauties

Wear these suits whether you intend to swim or not. Create a splash before you touch the water!

The Marlene
Slinky anthurium with Queen Anne's lace, grass twists, and polished pebbles.

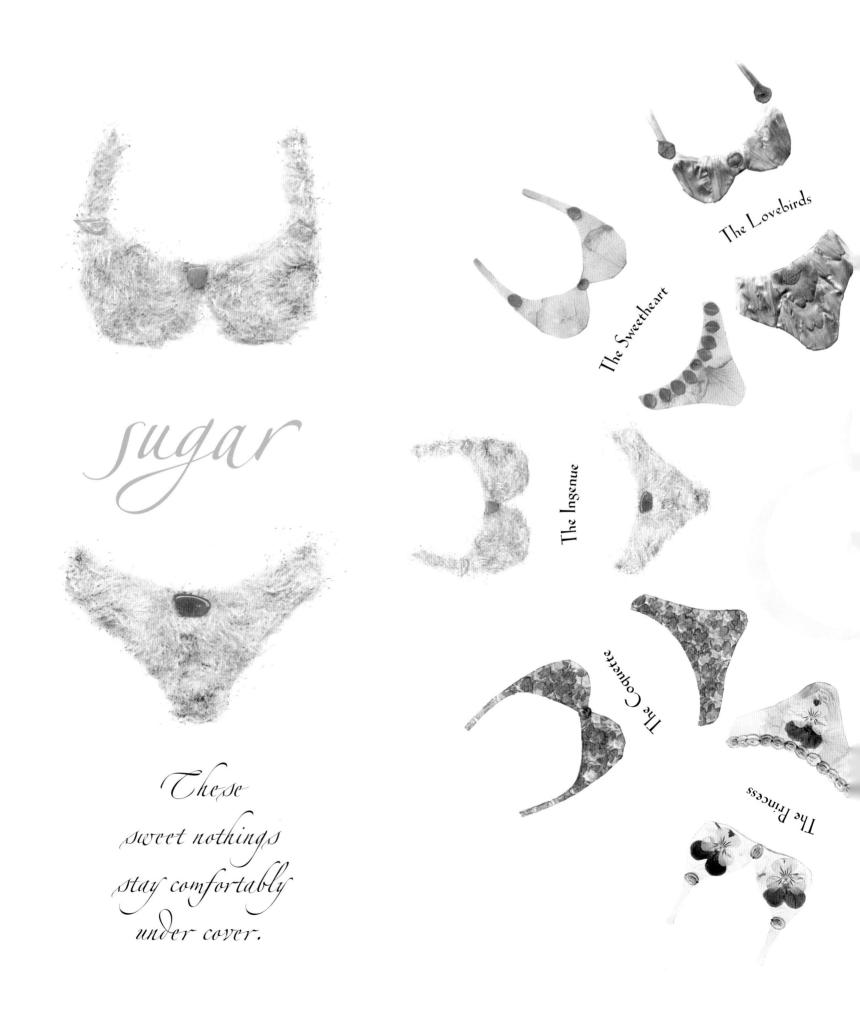

sugar

These
sweet nothings
stay comfortably
under cover.

The Lovebirds

The Sweetheart

The Ingenue

The Coquette

The Princess

The Gamine

The Femme Fatale

The Scamp

The Peacock

The Tomato

spice

These saucy
underpinnings
can't wait
to take the spotlight.

The Huntress
Leaf skeleton over crow feathers; pheasant trim
and peacock straps.

Well camouflaged, she spends
hours in the cattails watching

turtles and polliwogs,

newts and bullfrogs — an

avid huntress with her eyes.

There's a fairie who strolls every evening,
daringly on the same path. He walks in confidence, his jacket's
subtle texture blending perfectly with the ancient oaks and rendering him
practically invisible. Yet his step is sprightly, for he knows the interior of
his coat is anything but quiet and hints at
his own vibrant inner thoughts.

Oak Leaf Jacket

Oak leaves with aquilegia and
dandelion buttons. And of course,
the larkspur lining. For the male
fairie who laughs at labels.
Ample wing slots.

Artist's Smock

Clothe yourself with panache in calla lily petals. Only a fairie with integrity
can carry off this one — naturally, the buttons are made of honesty seeds.

Every aeon or so, a fairie comes along who doesn't give a fig for today's sense of fashion. Why should she? She's an artist. Although her creations bear no resemblance to what anyone else is wearing, somehow they convey that Her Choice is the correct one — and that everyone else has made a Terrible Mistake.

It's Now or Never

Put on your Top-Ten Topper
and picture yourself:
The stage is bare and
you're standing there—
with adoring fans all
around.
The King is back!

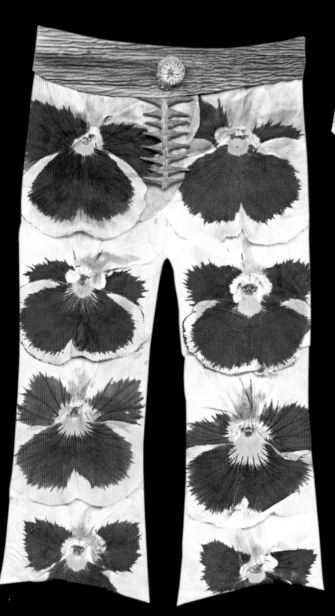

Aloha Jacket
Does your memory stray to the bright summer's day when you
first gazed upon the finest of all jackets? Calla lilies with
stargazer lining; viola and verbena trim with crystal buttons.

Let's Have a Party Pants
Pansy trousers, belted by a lily leaf, zipped by bracken,
and cinched with a daisy center button. They'll move with you,
no matter where the music moves you.

These Shoes Weren't Made for Walking
But that's OK, because they were made for flying.
For when you've kicked off your blue suedes and are heading
for the clouds. Pansies with daisy centers.

SASHAY
HIKE,
TIPTOE,
SCAMPER
DASH

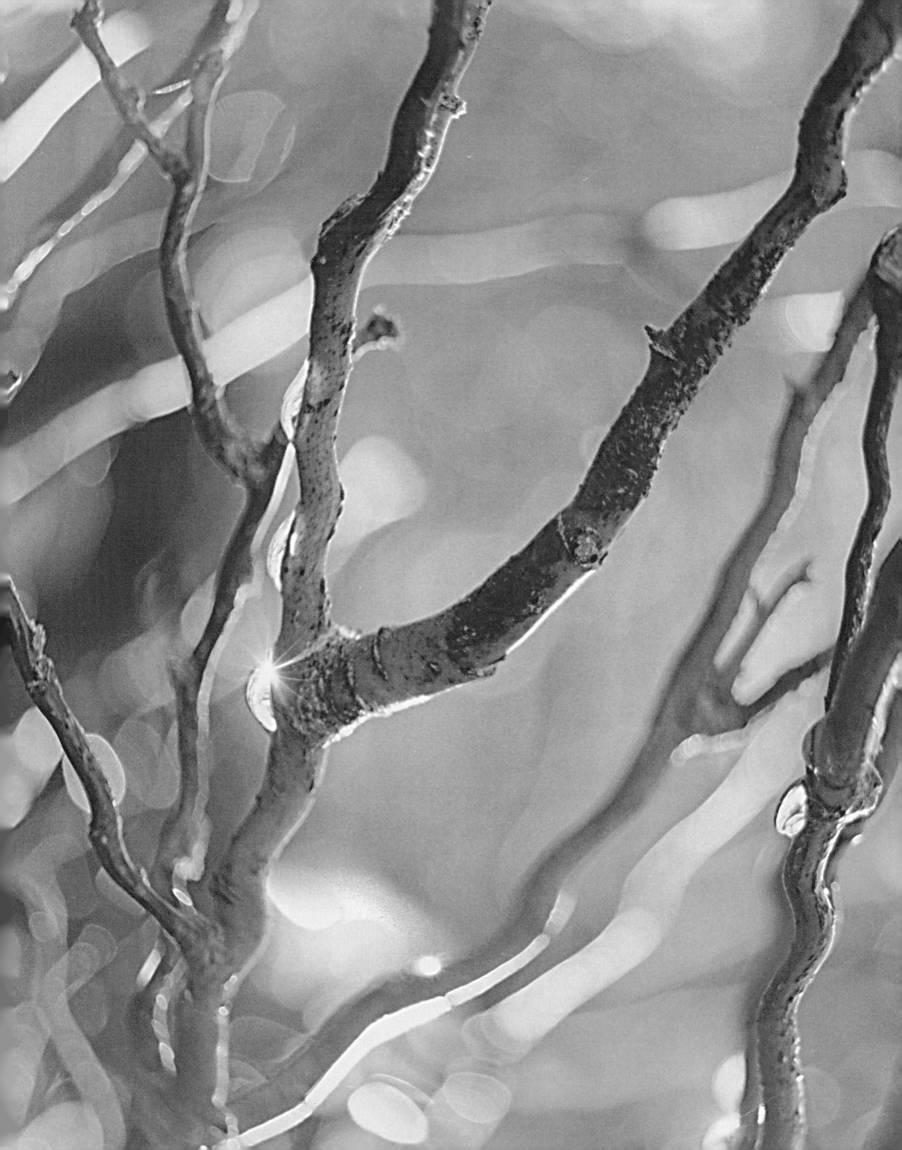

On tops of dewy grass

Nimbly do we pass,

The young and tender stalk

Ne'er bends when we do walk.

Yet in the morning may be seen

Where we the night before have been.

The Hot Heel

A spike sandal that shows some toe.
Silver birch soles with pheasant feathers
and a pine cone heel.

Tiptoe

The Balancing Act

Stilettos of birch bark covered in
skeleton leaf; yellowed grass strap and
a sprinkle of cow parsley seed.

Our flower petal slip-on flats
are elegant on earth, easily
removable for flight.
You'll want to pick
a bunch.

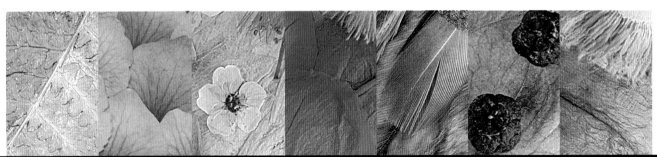

Bracken Green   Purple Hydrangea   Desert Marigold   Fiery Rose   Auburn Pheasant   Wild Mauve   Stargazer Pink

Fringed clam diggers sidle up to well-heeled, fringed pansy boots.

Pheasant feathers feature for both bell-bottoms and not-so-scruffy scuffs.

The Varsity

You didn't need a moment's thought about what to throw on for this date—you're a natural. Fifties-style rose petal coat with a sycamore standup collar.

Desert Boots

Heads will turn for a second look at these walk-on-water desert boots. Birch bark covered by leaf skeletons with a strand of peacock feather for a lace.

Flower Child

Rose petal shirt with a collar of
beech leaves and one delicious
orange cosmos, splashed just there.
We guarantee you'll get his attention.

Boss Boots

These are the "must have" boots
of The Season. Too bad they're
practically one-of-a-kind.
Rose petals with hot red verbena
and cool apache plume trim.

Mix & Match

The High & Flighty Hat

Top-Ten Topper

Pine Needle Shako

Worried about finding the right look? You'll flip for our mix-and-match. Play out your fantasies here on the page— and imagine them all coming true when that great big package from the new Ellwand catalogue arrives via special crow courier!

Daisy Tank

Oaken Camouflage Shirt

Cleopatra T-Shirt

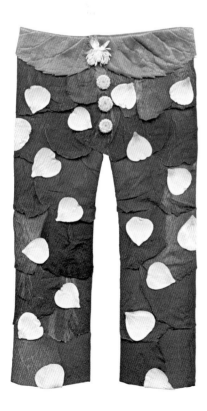

Elysium Trousers

Oaken Breeches

Hydrangea Hip-Huggers

Primary Plumed Shirt

The Blissful Tank

Cosmos Jacket

Primary Trousers

Pheasant Trunks

Rhubarb Skirt

Knee Deep in Pansies Trousers

Ring My Bell Bottoms

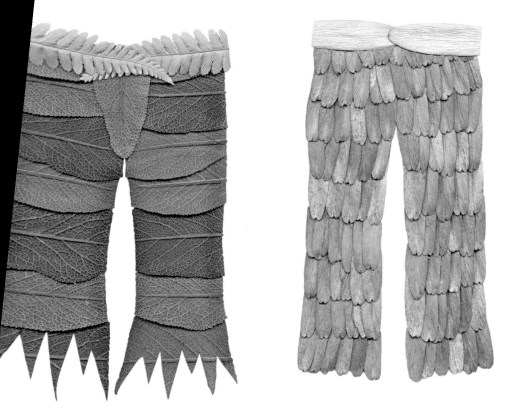

Fast Track Tank

Carnaby Shirt

Fill It to the Top Tank

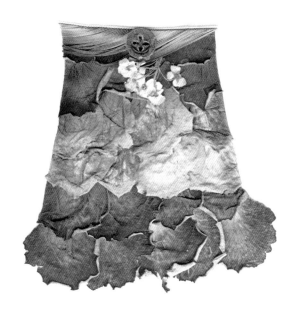

Ruffled Rose Mini

Uncommon Crow Trousers

Clam Diggers

Jester Jacket

Parrot Pop Top

Starry Night Shirt

Buttercup Beach Trousers

Snake Charmers

Garden of Eden Trousers

Fern Frond Mitre

Tippecanoe

Rose Pierrot

Ticket to Paradise T-shirt

Sunny Side Up Tank

Delphine Shirt

Dancing Dhotis

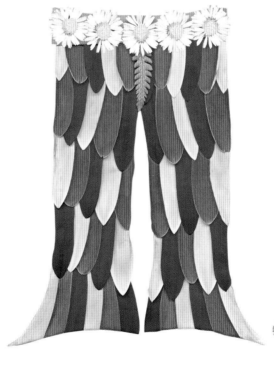

Harlequin Bell-Bottoms

Flared Flair A-Line

Flower Power

Harlequin Bell-Bottoms
Hip hip-huggers of gerbera petals with daisy belt and bracken zip.

"Are you kidding me?"
Nope.
If you're bold enough to handle it, press the petal to the metal and go from zero to one-eighty by taking flower power away from the ladies.
We prefer these hip concoctions without a shirt, but you decide how much of a stir you're prepared to create.

She Loves Me Jeans
Lily leaves and daisies; gerbera belt with forget-me-not—and we're sure they won't!

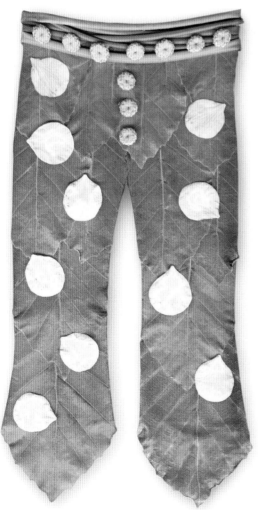

Garden of Eden Trousers
Beech leaves with buttercup petals; grass belt trimmed with dandelion.

Picture yourself after a starlit dinner by the sea. You are dancing barefoot in the sand. The night air and his arms are close around you — no need for a shawl. Suddenly he whispers in your ear . . . Will you . . .

The Bare Minimum

Wild geraniums and buttercups with narrow grass straps. Somehow you knew this would be the weekend that he would pop The Question.

Meet-the-Parents Day Dress

Rhododendron leaves with King Henry violas
and buttercups, daisy center buttons.
Time to share everything with your families and friends.

The Buttercup Beach Suit

Toreador pants with matching tank top, all of buttercup.
He loves you!
Now you'll make your wedding plans.

Bonfires flame on hilltops, their embers snapping and sparkling in the velvet sky. Thousands of fireflies gleam like tiny lanterns and spread the glow across the meadow for the bridal party and guests. The flower girls have been gently gathering peacock butterflies to release in a cloud just as Lydia makes her entrance through an archway of calla lilies. Could there be a more romantic time than Midsummer's Eve?

A Fairie Tale Wedding

Mother of the Bride

Just yesterday your little girl was flitting over

meadows and darting in and out of forest pools.

Is it possible that today

you will dress for her wedding?

Mother-of-the-Bride Hat

This glorious hat is fashioned of duck and goose. The pat on the head goes to you!

Mother-of-the-Bride Gown

This elegant and sophisticated gown of duck and goose feathers with snail shell buttons
blends drama and whimsy—a perfect expression of the woman you are.

The Cut-Above Crow Top Hat

A splendid tower of gleaming crow feathers
bound by snakeskin.

The Cut-Away Crow Jacket

The smoothest of crow feathers with a
dash of parrot at the lapel. Snail buttons and
epaulettes of pheasant, peacock, and shell
for the well-groomed husband-to-be.

Lily Bridesmaid

This year's colour, celadon green, was spirited straight from a sprite's underwater palace and is freshly interpreted in this flowing gown. The bodice of stargazer lilies is studded with a starlike poppy top, and the demure sleeves are also poppy. Evanescent.

The Maid of Honour

Silky crow feathers and a
single green parrot feather
gather in layers, creating the
touch-me velveteen look of
the skirt —spellbinding. The
bodice and straps are lily
leaves; the overbodice,
a whispering tracery
of skeleton leaf.
Sumptuous.

Flower Girl Gown

Parrot feathers and curls of lily
petals with the signature
Ellwand loop form the skirt.
Skeleton leaves overlay the
calla lily bodice, which has
puffed, love-in-the-mist sleeves
and a burst of bottle brush at
the neck. Any flower girl's
dream of a dress.

After releasing clouds of butterflies, the
flower girls continue spinning their magic,
scattering rose petals from
their glossy magnolia leaf baskets.

Here comes

the bride

I sing of feather gowns

and veils of air;

Of lilies for the

bride most fair.

Bridal wreath caplet with three diaphanous skeleton leaves.

Overlaid lily petal bodice with lily straps and rabbit's foot clover; heather flower and snail shell at the waist; skirt and train of calla lily, goose feather, and skeleton leaf.

Arise, my love, my fair one,

and come away;

for lo, the winter is past,

the rain is over and gone.

The flowers appear on the earth,

and the time of singing has come.

To the discerning
Ellwand eye,
beauty is everywhere.

Seeking the finest
and freshest materials,
Ellwand conducts
extensive gathering trips
on two continents and
enlists the help of
quality suppliers
worldwide.

Blossoms
Leaves
Petals
Seeds
Stems
Pods
Buds
Plumes
Shells
Feathers
Bark

Bark
Feathers
Shells
Plumes
Buds
Pods
Stems
Seeds
Petals
Leaves
Blossoms

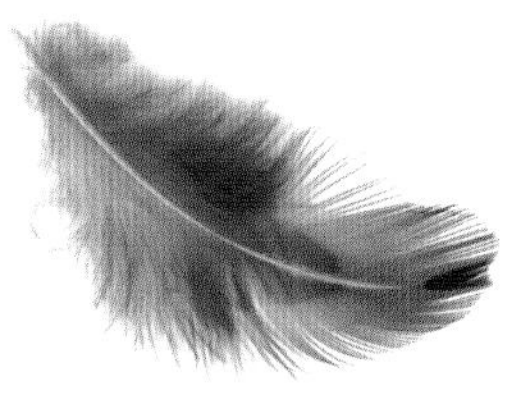

Pick-me-up passementerie

acorn top

Apache plume seed head

ash key seedpod

bullrush seed

Chinese lantern

cow parsley seed

cypress cone

honesty seed

pinecone

poppy top

red gum seed

shed snakeskin

Shells and stones

crystal

pebble

seashell

snail shell

stone

Plucked from the air

crow

duck

goose

jay

owl

parrot

partridge

peacock

pheasant

pigeon

From branch and vine

alder leaf

American oak leaf

bay leaf

beech leaf

birch bark

birch leaf

bracken fern

cedar bark

cotoneaster leaf

dock leaf

English oak leaf

fuchsia leaf

ivy leaf

lily leaf

monkey puzzle leaf

purple sage leaf

rhododendron leaf

rhubarb leaf

rose leaf

skeleton leaf

sweet chestnut leaf

sycamore leaf

variegated sage leaf

Found on the ground

grass

pine needles

thistle

thistledown

Coaxed from the earth

artichoke

crocus bulb

pumpkin

A flower by any name

anagallis

anthurium

aquilegia (columbine)

bluebell

bottlebrush flower

bougainvillaea

bridal wreath

buttercup

calla lily

cosmos

daisy

dandelion

delphinium

desert marigold

dianthus

forget-me-not

freesia

fritillary

fuchsia

gerbera daisy

heather blossom

hydrangea

Johnny-jump-up viola

King Henry viola

larkspur

lavender

lilac

Mexican bird of paradise

pansy

pincushion flower

Queen Anne's lace

rabbit-foot clover flower

rosebud and rose petal

shooting stars

stargazer lily

verbena

wild geranium

Please note that only regulated game and found feathers are used at the House of Ellwand.

The couturier extends thanks to the designers of this catalogue, art director Chris Paul and associate art director Ann Stott, for their empathy and expertise; copy writer Eugenie Bird for her enchanting lines; fashion illustrator David Downton for capturing the essence of the fairie form; technical assistant Gregg Hammerquist for his wizardry; editorial assistant Monica Perez for her magical powers of observation and organization; and my editor and publisher, Karen Lotz ("Hocus Pocus"), for her vision and support — without which there would be no Ellwand Collection.

I also would like to thank Alexis Banyon, Christine Corcoran Cox, Cecile Proverbs, Steve Thomas, Brandy Polay, and Lynn Gifford.

This catalogue was printed by Sing Cheong Printing Company, Ltd. in Hong Kong. The text stocks include Nopa matte, Tomohawk, and vellum, printed in four colours with two metallics and a press varnish. The jacket was printed in five colours with foil blocking and a spot UV, plus a matte laminate, on a Lumi gloss art. The endpapers are a woodfree stock. Separations and proofing were done by Bright Arts H.K., Ltd. in Hong Kong and GRB Editrice in Verona, Italy. The text was set in Zapfino, Eva Antiqua, and Cypress.

For my mother and father, and for Ruth and Lydia —D. E.

Credits

Page 18: "There sleeps Titania . . . a fairy in." William Shakespeare.
A MIDSUMMER NIGHT'S DREAM, 2.1.253-56.

Page 72: "On tops of dewy grass . . . have been." From Thomas Percy,
"Sportive Gambols" in REALMS OF MELODY, ed. Geoffrey Callender
(London: Macmillan & Co., Ltd., 1916).

Page 110: "Arise, my love . . . has come." Song of Solomon 1:10-12.

First published 2002 by Walker Books Ltd
87 Vauxhall Walk, London SE11 5HJ

This edition produced 2003 for
The Book People Ltd, Hall Wood Avenue,
Haydock, St Helens WA11 9UL

10 9 8 7 6 5 4 3 2 1

Text © 2002 Eugenie Bird
Artwork and photography © 2002 David Ellwand
Illustrations © 2002 David Downton

Printed in China

British Library Cataloguing in Publication Data:
a catalogue record for this book is available from the British Library

ISBN 0-7445-8065-X

www.walkerbooks.co.uk